Drama

Pamela Blackie, Bess Bullough and Doris Nash

Citation Press, New York 1972

ISBN 590-09526-9

Library of Congress Catalog Card number 76-174590

This book is published simultaneously in Great
Britain, Canada and other countries of the British
Commonwealth by Macmillan Education Ltd and
in the United States by Citation Press, Library
and Trade Division, Scholastic Magazines, Inc.

Cover photograph and photographs on pages 47–9
by courtesy of Henry Grant.

Designer Richard Hollis

Printed in the U.S.A.

Preface

The purpose of the Anglo-American Primary Education Project is to provide descriptions of the way that British primary schools work. They are published in this series of booklets under the general title of *Informal Schools in Britain Today* and they have been written for American and British educators and teachers-in-training as well as for the general public.

The authors are either practitioners or expert observers of British primary education and, in most cases, they document the work of the schools through detailed case examples; where it is relevant, implications are stated and conclusions drawn. It is not the intention to provide theoretical discussions or prescriptive manuals to informal education, but rather to present accounts from which deductions and generalizations can be made. In so doing, these booklets draw on the experience of that large minority of primary schools that have adopted informal methods.

It is hoped that the booklets will help educators who are looking for examples to substantiate change in particular schools and also those who are concerned, as teachers, educators or administrators, with the wider implications of the education of young children. For students who plan to become teachers these accounts of what happens in the classrooms of British primary schools provide ample material for discussion as well as helpful insights into the practice of teaching.

The series has been prepared under the aegis of the Schools Council in England with the support of the Ford Foundation in the United States. Planning was assisted by a small Anglo-American advisory group whose members are listed on page 4. The views expressed are however personal to each author.

3

British Directorate

Geoffrey Cockerill, Project Chairman/Joint Secretary, Schools Council for Curriculum and Examinations, London.

John Blackie/Formerly Chief Inspector, Primary Education, Department of Education and Science, London.

Molly Brearley/Formerly Principal, Froebel Institute College of Education, London

Maurice Kogan, Project Co-ordinator/Professor of Government and Social Administration, School of Social Sciences, Brunel University, Uxbridge, Middlesex.

American Participants

J. Myron Atkin/Dean, School of Education, University of Illinois, Urbana, Illinois.

Ann Cook/Co-director, Community Resources Institute, 270 W. 96th Street, New York.

Joseph Featherstone/Writer; Lecturer, John Fitzgerald Kennedy School of Government, Institute of Politics, Harvard University, Cambridge, Massachusetts.

Professor David Hawkins/Director, Mountain View Center for Environmental Education, University of Colorado, Boulder, Colorado.

Herb Mack/Co-director, Community Resources Institute, 270 W. 96th Street, New York.

Marjorie Martus/Program Officer, The Ford Foundation, New York, N.Y.

Casey Murrow/Teacher, Wilmington Elementary School, Wilmington, Vermont.

Liza Murrow/Antioch-Putney Graduate School of Education, Putney, Vermont.

Mary Lela Sherburne/Director, Pilot Communities Project, Education Development Center, Newton, Mass.

Contents

The Authors

Doris Nash has done social work in a poor urban area with mothers and babies, and has cared for children with physical and emotional handicaps. Later she trained as a teacher. After eight years' work in a very old school, she was appointed headteacher of Sea Mills Infant School, Bristol, where the constant aim of the staff is to meet the children's need for all round development.

Pamela Blackie trained at the Royal Academy of Dramatic Art and has the University of London Diploma in Dramatic Art. At the outbreak of war she became Drama Adviser for the Yorkshire Rural Community Council, and was later Drama Adviser for the Council for the Encouragement of Music and the Arts (which became the Arts Council). She was later Adviser for the Community Council of Lancashire. In the 1950s, she wrote and produced many plays, mainly religious drama. She also taught drama in a boys' Borstal. She is author of A DRAMA TEACHER'S HANDBOOK (Blackwell, 1956). She now teaches drama, part-time, at Huntingdon County Primary School.

Bess Bullough taught in various schools from 1934, first as a general class teacher, and later specializing in English, drama and physical education. She became interested in the Movement approach to physical education and creative work, and experimented in the relationship between movement, sound and speech. During the past twenty years, she has demonstrated and lectured on this work to training college students and at in-service courses. She has made teaching films for the West Riding authority and the BBC, and video tapes for training colleges. In 1968, she received the MBE, for work in the educational field. She is currently head of department for physical education and drama in a middle school in the West Riding of Yorkshire.

Introduction

Until fairly recently, school drama in England was largely confined to secondary schools. In particular, the big grammar schools in London, and some of the independent boarding schools, have a tradition going back to the beginning of this century or earlier. In primary schools, however, drama has been limited, with few exceptions, to a Christmas Nativity play from a printed script and to a rather half-hearted feature known as Dramatization found chiefly in infant schools. In the last decade, however, there has been a great quickening of life and much innovation in primary school drama, affecting a substantial minority of schools all over the country.

It is not easy to be sure of the influences which have been at work behind this movement, but two at least can be identified. The arrival in England of a wartime refugee from Hitlerism, Rudolph Laban, stimulated practical interest in his theories, and an increasing number of schools do a subject which they call Movement. The object of Movement in school is to provide a basic training in control of the body so that all movements may be improved, and so that the specialized movements required for particular sports and crafts may be more easily learned. Movement is as much the basis of dance, ballet, and drama as it is of football, swimming, and ski-ing, and Movement in the Laban sense has developed in an artistic direction as well as in a more purely acrobatic one. It is a curious fact that, while Laban's influence in the USA has been mainly in the professional theatre, displayed in particular in the distinguished work of Martha Graham, in England it has been almost entirely in schools. Much of the most interesting dramatic work going on at present in English primary schools follows the Laban principles very closely, and nearly all of it is affected by them.

A second influence has been that of the drama advisers. The first advisers had nothing to do with schools and indeed were forbidden to enter them. They were appointed early in the Second World War by the Council for the Encouragement of Music and the Arts and by the various Community Councils, to stimulate adult and youth drama as a contribution to civilian morale. Some ten years ago, however, they were transferred to the local education authorities with a responsibility which included schools. Some of the older advisers whose experience had been confined to older age-groups had little to offer the primary schools but, increasingly, they and their successors have become interested in drama for young children and, for the first time, professional skill and knowledge has been available to the teachers. The appointment, by the Department of Education and Science, of a Staff Inspector of Drama, in 1953, confirmed the growing importance attached to the subject by educational opinion.

These two influences have operated, so far as primary schools are concerned, mainly upon individual teachers who have initiated dramatic activity in their own classes, and who often seem to hold very strong views about how it should be done, and even stronger views about how it should not be done. Those who are strong adherents of the Laban Movement believe that children must begin by a purely physical approach, and learn the use and control of their bodies without any appeal to the imagination. Only when they have advanced a considerable distance along the road of physical mastery should they be allowed to use their imaginations. 'You must never *be* an old man,' they will say. 'You must move *like* an old man.' Others would argue that children will use their imaginations, whether the teacher likes it or not, and that the imagination provides one means of learning to move.

It is not necessary to follow out this argument here, but it explains the composition of this booklet which differs from all the others in the series in that it consists of separate contributions by three different teachers. Each has evolved, not of course uninfluenced by others, but essentially for herself, a method and practice for dramatic work with young children. Each has written in her own manner, an account of what she does with her children, and two have given some indication of how they came to adopt their present practices. No attempt has been made to harmonize the three contributions, though it will be noticed that, despite some differences in approach, there is a great deal of common ground between them. Each eschews public performance. Each uses the whole floor space and will have nothing to do with a conventional stage. Each brings the whole class rather than a selected cast into the work. Each makes a maximum use of movement, with words coming slowly and at a later stage. None has any use for a play, in the sense of something written for children by an adult and published. All three, to a varying extent, link the dramatic work with other activities and experiences which go on in the school.

It must be stated, in conclusion, that there are schools in England where the dramatic work does not fit with what is described in this booklet. The initiative and independence of each individual teacher is no myth and those who wish to do formal production of scripted plays are at perfect liberty to do it. Here and there will be found very gifted teachers who make a success of this, though, it must be added, always at the cost of leaving out the majority of the children and using only 'the good actors'. However, it would seem that it is the type of work described in this booklet which represents the most interesting and the most important development in progress today.

John Blackie

1 Drama in the Junior School

by Pamela Blackie

I started teaching drama in a junior school eight years ago. Some children asked me to do it, and with their headmaster's consent I began by teaching a drama club in the school outside lesson time. After a term, it was decided that drama could be included in the curriculum, so I was able to do it in school hours. The experience I had to draw on when I started was a professional dramatic training, a university diploma in dramatic art, a brief time in professional repertory, a number of years taking drama classes for adults and teenagers, and the production of plays (some written by myself— dramatized folk tales, poems, and bible stories) among children, at home, in the village where I live, and on occasion in the neighbouring town.

The school contains nearly 600 children. It is one of two junior schools which serve a small but growing county town in a predominantly rural county. Most of the classes I take have about forty children in them, but usually I take half the class at a time for thirty minutes. I teach only one day a week, and classes I take have age ranges of seven to eight, eight to nine, and ten to eleven.

I made a great many mistakes when I started. I produced scenes with the children in a formal manner which I now think more suitable for boys and girls in secondary schools. I imposed my own idea of what was dramatic on them, rather than letting them try out their ideas of what was dramatic on me, which is what I try to do now. Very fortunately, I never made the mistake of boring them, so I was able to go on experimenting. Now, by a process of trial and error, the drama I teach has become an activity in which the children act for their own sake and for the sake of each other, not for the purpose of interesting an audience.

The other day I watched, unseen, some six-year-olds in their school playground. One discovered the cover of a drain; he beckoned to a companion and pointed, and the two looked at the cover; then the second boy picked up an imaginary key, fitted it into place and, using his whole bodily strength, turned the key. He then replaced the key on the ground and, in imagination, lifted the cover. It must have been heavy, for the muscles in his arms and shoulders came up. He put it on the ground, and then both boys knelt down and peered into the hole. By that time, other children in the playground had begun to watch them and to talk to each other about what they were doing. Then one boy rolled up his sleeve and put his arm into the imaginary hole (he had in fact to bend his arm flat over the ground as the real cover was still in place); he got up with an imaginary something in his hand and showed it to the other boy; they peered over it with their heads together. At this point, the rest of the children gathered round to look too, and the end of the story was lost to view as far as I was concerned.

I have described this incident in detail because it seemed to me to be a perfect example of the imaginative play, completely absorbing and real, on which one is building in teaching drama to children. The idea was suggested by a physical object, the cover of a drain. Some of the imaginary experiences involved in playing it out were physical: the effort of turning the key, the effect of lifting something heavy, the feeling around a hole in the ground. There were also emotional experiences involved: curiosity, determination to find out, and the excitement of discovery. The whole thing was essentially dramatic. The first boy saw the cover, called his friend, and pointed at it. There was no seeing, calling, and pointing, all at the same time, which is what children—and many adults—do when acting a character. The whole thing built itself up to the climax of discovery, the other children in the playground playing perfectly the part of all crowds in dramatic scenes, gradually becoming more and more involved, and then gathering round the principals at the climax. All this was completely spontaneous and unproduced.

Planning a drama class Drama then, must involve deeply the child's imagination, his body and his emotions, and it must be acceptable to his mind as well, which means that the experiences suggested to him must be suitable to his age and state of development. I did not, and do not, positively think of this when planning material for a drama class, but I think that the most successful work, when the children have been truly involved and absorbed, has been achieved when the material has measured up to such requirements.

When planning a first encounter with children who have not done drama before, I try to bring into it, first, the imaginative physical experiences, then the imaginative emotional experiences, and then to draw on both in working them into some kind of dramatic scene. The following was the scheme I used for a group of nine-year-olds who had not done this kind of drama before.

Lie down on the floor. Curl up into a ball. Make yourselves as small and tight as you can. Now stretch out and relax.

Now, with your feet on the ground, curl up into a ball, tightly. Leap into the air as high as you can! Curl up again. Now relax.

Next, I take falls and stabbing. I show all the children the technique of falling without hurting themselves; then, after they have all tried falling, they get into pairs, and A stabs B while B falls. In the course of this, they discover that, if you are going to try to hurt someone (ie, stab him), you must first hate him, and that hatred makes your body go stiff and tense all over, in the way it does when you are curled up tightly in a ball; also, that, at the touch of the stab, the victim goes stiff with shock but that he must relax quickly before he falls. They find these discoveries interesting. They find that the hatred has an element of 'menace' in it. This is a word that always seems to crop up sooner or later in improvised drama. Younger juniors usually don't know what it means, the first time they hear it, but they subsequently use it a good deal themselves.

Next I say something like this:

Now you can tighten all your muscles till you feel very strong. Make a slow, strong movement. How can you make a slow strong movement which is also 'menacing'?

At this point, one of the children will sometimes have something to say about why you might feel 'menacing' towards somebody else.

We then talk about the 'reaction' to menacing movements.

If someone bigger and stronger than you made a slow menacing movement, what would you do?—show me!

The response is usually fear, expressed by the quick nervous form of movement.

Now, show me slow, strong, menacing movements, with your partner reacting with quick nervous movements.

Gradually, the slow movements become more threatening and the quick movements more frightened.

Now let's make two groups; one group is strong, fierce and menacing, the other is intimidated and fearful.

Then I tell them:

Four of you are rich people with food and money; the rest of you are poor and starving. How do you poor people feel about the rich ones? And what do you rich people feel about the poor ones?

They tell me.

Now, let's plan a scene with a climax.

(This is another word which sometimes needs explanation, but which they will use a lot in future.)

The poor people are sitting in the street, hungry and hopeless; they see the rich people coming; they approach them; they beg, beseech, cajole, and finally threaten, all to no avail; the proud, frightened, rich people hurry past them as quickly as possible, and the poor people sink down again, disappointed and apathetic.

We usually do this scene twice and, as this is the first day, we leave it there. But if this same scene were used with more experienced children, they would divide up into groups, discuss it, and perhaps use words, beginning with murmurs of resentment, developing into shouted abuse, and dying away into bitterness.

Using emotions It has been pointed out to me that this scheme for a first lesson makes great use of violence and feelings of hatred, and I have been asked whether I don't think that I am encouraging the children to behave in a violent way towards each other, and towards other people. My answer is that the feelings of hatred and violence are there already, somewhere inside the children, and they had much better bring them out and learn to handle their emotions legitimately, in the drama class, than discover them for the first time under the stress of real anger and bitterness.

15

The above are strong emotions, easy to discover in oneself, but they are not the only feelings it is possible to make use of at the beginning. This was another first lesson for a similar group of children:

Another first lesson
Lie down on the floor, completely relaxed, so that you feel the floor is holding you up. There is a nice warm fire beside you; you are relaxed like a cat; you are a cat. Stretch yourself! Now, move away somewhere else in the room . . . now relax again. Now—someone throws cold water at you!

At this point, a number of the children jumped up, arched their backs and spat, and then stalked away—those who didn't, soon got the idea from the others.

Now you are yourself again. Lie down and bask in the sun. A cold wind begins to blow; the wind is getting stronger; you begin to walk; as you walk, the wind gets stronger—and stronger—and stronger! It begins to snow; the snow comes down over your hair and into your collar, onto your eyebrows; you take shelter with your back against a wall; the snow goes whirling by; you begin to grow numb . . . to freeze. You freeze until you are an iceberg, and you can't move hand or foot. Then the wind drops, the sun comes out; you begin to feel again; your muscles straighten out; your fingers and toes hurt, but you can move your arms and legs. Feel them! They belong to you again! Now the sun gets hotter and hotter; you can hardly lift your arms and legs, they are so feeble. You can't stand any more; you collapse and relax.

This meteorological fantasy, and the 'getting under the skin of' a cat, are experiences of bodily relaxation and tension, and the way in which circumstances affect these. In the 'weather' lesson, we went on to discuss other weather situations.

You have just experienced walking in a buffeting wind; how about other things which you may have to do in a wind?

The girls try out unpegging and bringing in washing from a line; the boys try bringing a boat ashore and making her fast. Then, the boys become fishermen in a storm, and the girls become fishermen's wives waiting on the cliff top. The class ends with the children sitting down in pairs; the boys telling each other how worried they were that they wouldn't be able to get to the shore, and the girls talking about their anxiety that the fishing boats might be lost and the men drowned. This prepares the way for the next class, which might involve making up a scene about a shipwreck, or a cliff rescue, or some other happening with a wind and sea setting.

Starting from the physical In planning a drama class, I try to make the beginning a physical rather than an emotional experience; emotions creep in inevitably, since all physical experiences must have some degree of pleasantness or unpleasantness about them, but the aim is to give the children something to limber up on, something which, if possible, can be used in a dramatic scene taken later on in the lesson. Here are some examples of beginnings:

You are seaweed, draped over a rock, which rises and falls with the tide.

You are in a room where the walls and floor have magnetic currents which can be switched on and off.

You are marionettes with strings attached to your head, back, wrists, and feet. You are completely floppy until I pull your strings.

You are candles (or matches) which someone lights (or strikes), and you burn down.

You are a mechanical toy which can be wound up, and which stops when the clockwork runs down.

You are a Jack-in-the-Box which is set off, and then put back in a box.

With your partner: one of you is a kite, the other is the person who puts the kite together and then flies it.

With your partner: one of you is 'Action Man' and the other the person who tries out the various attitudes 'Action Man' can assume.

You are running after someone, when he suddenly produces Medusa's head and turns you to stone in the attitude of running.

You are a spaceman arriving on a planet with little or no gravity.

An imagined situation

The main part of each drama class is usually concerned with some imagined situation, which may be something in itself or may be developed into a more elaborate scene.

It is difficult to select examples of imaginative situations because the possibilities are so numerous and varied. Literally almost anything is possible, but the best scenes happen when the children build up the situation themselves.

You are in a wood at night, what can you hear?
The children say: *Owls, wind in the trees, branches creaking, twigs cracking, leaves scuffling.*

Oh—what time of year is it then?
Autumn—we can hear wolves howling.

Where is this wood then?
In some mountains where there are wolves. It is beginning to snow. We are walking by lantern light, and the wolves see the lantern and follow us. They stand among the trees watching us, with their eyes

glittering in the moonlight. We run and run, and then we see the light of a cottage in the distance. We run through the wood, falling over the roots of trees, and reach the cottage door, and bang on it. We're exhausted! The woman inside is frightened and doesn't open the door at first, but after a bit she lets us in just before the wolves catch us. It's warm in the cottage, and then we faint with exhaustion on the hearth rug.

By now the scene is well under way, and full of possibilities. With an inexperienced class, I should encourage them to act it in pairs, one partner being the traveller escaping from the wolves and the other the woman in the cottage. With an experienced class, some children would probably be trees in the forest, animated trees that claw at the traveller, and others would be the pursuing wolves. In a class new to drama, the 'wolves' will always catch the 'travellers' and bite them—often, to begin with, working off private feuds in the process! But usually, a general feeling in the class that 'it spoils the story' prevents this happening again.

Disasters The dramatic possibilities of disasters such as earthquakes, erupting volcanoes, shipwrecks, fires, floods and avalanches are obvious. To begin with, the children usually act them out as themselves, or else as a group of people such as fishermen, peasants, or explorers, but after a time the portrayal of character can be introduced.

The gentle old man who returns to find his cottage flattened by an earthquake and his family dead in the ruins—how about him, does he accept it with resignation or does he curse God for letting it happen?

The twisted avaricious old man who returns to find that the earthquake has buried his bag of gold deep in the ground, and that from now on he must be dependent on the charity of the neighbours he has neglected and despised; how about him?

An emotion With older juniors a situation can sometimes be evolved by thinking about an emotion such as loneliness, homesickness, anxiety, temptation or fear. The boy or girl returning after an air raid to a house that has been destroyed by bombing may experience utter loneliness as he/she sits among the ruins, thinking of the days when this was a home. But loneliness implies that the family are dead; if they may be alive somehow, somewhere, then anxiety must be the main emotion, because anxiety is connected with hope. This is sometimes discovered in a drama class. Usually, quite early on, children will make up a scene which involves a clash between 'good' people and 'bad' people, and will discover that the 'bad' people are always the more convincing and interesting. Why? 'Because', said one inspired boy aged ten, 'You can't just be good by yourself; you can only be good *to* someone.' After that, the scene had to be replanned, and the 'good' people given objects for their charity.

Other sources of drama The seasons and festivals of the year give plenty of scope for dramatic situations, particularly Hallowe'en with its legends and witches. Beginning the class by 'being a cat', as described earlier, (or any other suitable 'familiar') makes a good preparation for a story involving witches.

Another way that I find fruitful in getting children to build up a situation is to take a number of objects and give them to groups of children. I gave an old fox fur to a group of boys; they put it in the middle of the room: then, from all four corners, they stalked it, and finally killed it by stabbing! The same fur, given to a group of girls, was tried on, passed from hand to hand and, finally, quarrelled over. A brooch I brought in was 'valuable' because it contained (a) real diamonds, (b) smuggled drugs, (c) a secret agent's message, and (d) because of the person who gave it. It was lost or stolen, and found (a) buried in the garden, (b) in the churchyard, (c) in the crop of a chicken, and (d) in Piccadilly Circus on Eros' left ear.

Music I often use music to suggest ideas, to start the children limbering up at the beginning, and either to create or to enhance a situation during the main part of the class. Since I am not a musician, I am obliged to use music which has not been written specifically for this purpose, and which, therefore, is being to some degree misused in being employed to stir and canalize emotion in a drama class. I try to use music which is appropriate to what we are doing, and which I consider to be good of its kind—and, if it is any consolation to a musician reading this, many of the children have learned to enjoy listening to composers such as Debussy and Stravinsky because they originally heard them in the drama class. Music greatly helps a child to feel his own emotion in a situation, without being embarrassed by it. For example, Ravel's PAVANE FOR A DEAD INFANTA has helped many children mourning a dead kitten, or even being Hans Andersen's dying Little Match Girl, to weep real tears without any sense of incongruity or any desire to giggle.

Using speech In the drama class, using speech as a vital part of a scene sometimes presents difficulties. In my class, one of the more successfully evolved situations using speech occurred as follows. The children were concerned with the state of the fishing trawlers, and were sitting in pairs, discussing the conditions of work and the state of the boats, the boys as trawlermen, the girls as their wives. At my suggestion, and unknown to the other members of the class, one of the boys, who was a natural leader, got up and said loudly, 'It's no good just talking. Come on, men, we've got to do something about it!' The boys and girls all looked at him for a few seconds of stunned surprise, then another boy got to his feet and said, 'Yeah, we've got to do something.' Then a girl shouted, 'And about time too!' After this, a thoroughly lively scene was under way, the children generally all talking together, though occasionally a leader topped the others with his or her voice. When I broke up the scene, ten minutes later, to discuss it with them, several of them said in tones of surprise, 'I say, that was *fun!*'

I find that, until children are fairly experienced in improvised drama, to suggest improvised conversation between individuals tends to make for self-consciousness, which in its turn produces charades instead of drama. Occasionally, charades have their place in the drama class. Very often the children want to act stories of their own making, and it seems to me to be wrong to prevent their doing this simply because it produces a charade situation. The children often become conscious of this situation themselves, and one has to guide them through it, or take them back to spontaneous crowd scenes or improvised acting in pairs, until they are more self-confident.

The study of an emotion, referred to earlier, led to a scene involving spontaneous speech. In this case the emotion was homesickness; the class was a group of ten- and eleven-year-olds. I did not make any suggestions for the use of speech. The situation began with the children talking together, in pairs, about occasions in their own lives when they had been homesick. Then they became a group of refugee children in a strange country. I waited to see what would happen. A girl, self-appointed as a leader, stood up and said, 'Let's go home!'

'Yes, let's!' said the others.

'How can we do it?' she asked. From a spontaneous series of suggestions, a plan for creeping out of an orphanage at night and crossing a frontier unseen was evolved, and this they proceeded to act.

Extent of children's contribution

I think that a drama class should aim at handing over as much as possible to the children, and that, by the time they are about to leave the junior school, they should have a good deal of say in what they do in their classes. I find that, at this stage, they have a great many ideas for situations and scenes, and are prepared to write these down so that they can be acted in class. They usually want to have some kind of an 'occasion' before they leave school, which, if the drama that we did were suitable for an audience, would take the form of a performance to their parents. Since they are all agreed that our drama is not meant primarily for an audience, they usually invite their parents to an open drama class at which they act scenes and situations that they have planned out beforehand. In order that they should not start off in too self-conscious a 'state', we sometimes begin by using the audience in the scene. For example, the children planned out a scene about a witch hunt, in which their parents, from their seats round the room, joined in the hue and cry, 'She's a witch!', 'Burn her!', etc. The witch was then burned at the stake, some of the children being the fire that killed her, and the whole audience, children and parents alike, being the crowd watching the execution.

Evaluating work

I have been asked how I would evaluate a year's work with a class; what signs I would look for that would assure me that it had been, on the whole, a success. One of my first assurances is my own feeling in the class. For instance, to begin with, I had disciplinary difficulties, I was obliged to supply most of the ideas myself, and to keep a very tight hand on the class, or they would have been not only very noisy, but 'all over the place' as well. Towards the end of the year, the older juniors, at least, took more and more responsibility for the class themselves; they saw to it that the odd disruptive child was kept in his place, and I was consequently able to relax, and to be much more observant.

I would next try to judge just how involved the children had been in what they were doing. I have found that not every class is equally successful, and that things like the weather, the children's state of health, and tension over exams at the end of term,[1] or the lack of such tension, affect them. I have found that material which is tremendously absorbing to one group of children will leave another group comparatively cold, so that is is necessary to abandon it and try something else.

[1] The Selective Examination (eleven-plus) still exists in certain areas and also some schools set internal examinations

The most successful classes have been those where the children have developed and worked out an idea for themselves, and have become completely involved in it. This has usually been in some intensely human situation, such as the loss of a home through disaster, or the death of a dearly loved animal (the death of a person being too dreadful to contemplate dramatically), or in some entirely fantastic situation such as the discovery of strange animals, or unexplored country, or the putting of a curse on someone. The more involved the children become, the greater is their creative experience and this manifests itself in their growing more ready to show initiative in coming forward with useful ideas, in taking over the running of the class, and in disciplining themselves in it. They also show a greater sympathy towards all kinds of people and circumstances and, in their criticisms, the gradual evolution of a scale of values.

2 Basic and Expressive Movement

A World of Action, Thought and Feeling

by Bess Bullough

I started my teaching as an English and drama specialist in a senior school (age range, eleven to fifteen years). To me, then, drama meant a stage, acting techniques and an audience. I taught the techniques, set standards, and demanded results. I produced and directed well-ordered plays. The results were pleasing to me at that time, but I realize now that the majority of the children were never wholly involved, and that very little contribution was made to their growth and development.

From the senior school, I went to a mixed junior school (age range, three to eleven-plus), as a general class teacher. This school is situated in one of the most depressing areas of a mining town. The district served by the school is some two miles from open country, and there are no open spaces where the children can play. The district is in the shadow of two chemical works, a gas works and a colliery. The houses are small, were erected eighty to a hundred years ago, and are now slums. Some of them are being cleared, and their occupants moved to new housing estates, but most of the children attending the school live in slum conditions.

We had to find some means of bringing colour and vitality into this grey world; ways of making the school an exciting place where there was pride in achievement, and of helping the children to become more aware of their surroundings, and so increasing their sensitivity. We were eager to do anything that invited the children's involvement as feeling, thinking beings. So we concentrated on physical education, drama, music and art.

I began to experiment and explore the possibilities of a 'movement' approach to physical and creative education. The following are some of the observations and experiences which are the result of working in this way with the children at this junior school.

Basic movement

Every movement we make, moving part of the body or all the body, involves three basic fundamentals —the use of space, weight and time.

Space Use of much space, little space
Moving at different levels
Moving directly, moving indirectly

Time Moving at various speeds—moving quickly, slowly, coming to stillness, being still, leaving stillness

Weight Control of weight
Transfer of weight
Relaxation

Expressive movement

Expressive movement develops from exploring and experimenting with these basic fundamentals.

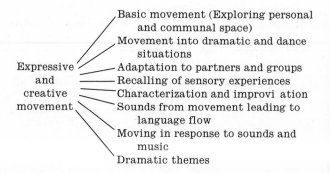

Expressive and creative movement
— Basic movement (Exploring personal and communal space)
— Movement into dramatic and dance situations
— Adaptation to partners and groups
— Recalling of sensory experiences
— Characterization and improvi ation
— Sounds from movement leading to language flow
— Moving in response to sounds and music
— Dramatic themes

Introducing movement

The first introduction to basic movement must be approached with patience and understanding. Instructions must be simple and clear, given in words the children can easily understand. The children must not be rushed into situations that are beyond their understanding or control. The awareness, self-discipline and control at which we are aiming cannot be expected from the start. If the movement experience is to be of real value, helping a child to become a *feeling* as well as a *thinking* being, then this must be a gradual process. The teacher must be prepared to accept what the children offer and then, through her observations, present them with situations that invite their interest, capture their imagination, and encourage their exploration, so helping them to become fully involved in what they are doing.

Throughout all the children's movement and dramatic experiences, they should be given frequent opportunities for observing each other's work. If this 'watching each other' is introduced sympathetically by the teacher, the children will accept it readily, and soon will comment on and discuss what they see. This class observation is of great value, for it helps to increase a child's awareness, clarify his movements, and deepen and widen his experience.

Exploration of personal and communal space

When I begin to work with a class of children who have had no previous movement experience, I first ask them to move about the hall in any way they choose. Invariably there is chaos and confusion. So we come to a halt. Then I ask the children each to find a space of his own where he is not touching anyone. Now I draw the children's attention to their own *personal space*. It could be in the following way:

We are each standing in our own space. Let's look at it. How much space have we to move in without touching anyone? Look right up to the ceiling and down to the floor. That space is yours. Stretch out as far as you can in all directions without touching anyone or 'stealing' anyone's space.

Now, move in any way you like in your own space *but take great care that you don't touch anyone else.*

At this stage of exploration, a child's movements will have little control or inner effort—it is just a game, which at this stage is right. But, from this stage, a child should be helped to become more aware of his own movements, to work with increasing control and absorption. Here I find it helpful to narrow the field of movement by directing the child's attention to one part of his body: eg, feet.

Look at your feet. Move them anywhere in your own space. Try standing on your toes, heels, sides of your feet. Watch your feet all the time. See how they move. Feel *how they move. Can you move your feet at different speeds? Sometimes quickly, sometimes slowly?*

Now try touching the floor lightly with your feet— anywhere in your space. Watch them carefully. Are you using all the space around you?

Can you let your feet sink into the floor . . . hit the floor? Can you feel the difference right from inside when they touch, sink into, or hit the floor?

Now explore your space with your feet, sometimes touching, sometimes sinking into, and sometimes hitting the floor. See how many different ways you can move your feet—but all the time watch how they are moving, feel *how they are moving.*

Here, and throughout all their movement experiences, the children should be given plenty of time to explore, select and consolidate. They will become more and more interested in watching and feeling what their feet can do. Their minds begin to direct their movements with increasing absorption, inner effort and control.

Now, return to further exploration of communal space. Ask the children to move around the hall again, finding for themselves how many different ways they can move on their feet. Remind them that wherever they go they must think of their own individual space, taking care not to touch or 'steal' anyone else's space. Now narrow the field again by giving definite instructions: eg, walking at varying speeds, looking for spaces; running in a straight line, and making a sudden stop (*feeling* the suddenness of the stop); running on a curving path, gradually getting slower until stillness is reached (*feeling* the stillness), and so on. After repeated moving around in this way, awareness of others in the group is increased, and moving with ease and control without invading another's territory becomes a habit.

Now, return to further exploration of personal space, perhaps this time concentrating on *transfer of weight*, aiming at increasing body management and flow. Remind the children that, so far, we have been moving mainly with our weight on our feet. Now we are going to experiment, taking our weight on other parts of our bodies—big parts and little parts: eg, hands, feet, back.

Stand perfectly still, so that you know your weight is on your feet. Think about lying down in your space. Now find out how slowly and smoothly you can get there. Feel the slowness and smoothness from inside as you are moving. Where is your weight now? Can you put your weight onto another part of your body? Think where it is going and then try moving it there quickly. Can you hold it there? Now relax so that every part of you sinks into the floor.

As you are lying there, think of two or three different parts where you could take your weight. Now, find a good starting place and work out each transfer, separately if you like, but somewhere trying to bring in quickness, slowness, and stillness. Now, repeat the same movements, trying to join the three transfers easily and smoothly into one sequence.

Here the children have been concerned mainly with controlling their movements in varying degrees of time. At the same time they will have been working at different spatial levels and in different directions, since it is impossible to isolate the fundamentals. During these movement sequences, without being actively aware of it, the children will have experienced different qualities of movement: eg, curling, stretching, and so on.

Awareness of movement qualities

To help the children to become consciously aware of these movement qualities, I introduce them to what I call 'shape-making'. They start by simply moving in their space to make shape patterns. They draw on previous movement experiences, using varying speeds, tensions, levels, and directions. They are invited to think about the movement qualities in the shapes they are making.

They readily make and feel the different movements in changing from a small, curled shape to a big stretching shape, finding different levels and directions within their own space. Other movement shapes can be suggested and explored: eg, a big, flowing movement, followed by a quick, straight movement, or a slow, strong movement, followed by quick, jerky movements. The children will soon begin to experiment on their own, letting their shapes flow from one into another. Through continued exploration and repetition, they begin to appreciate difference in movement qualities. Their work becomes increasingly expressive and, depending on how they feel, their shapes move towards dramatic and dance forms.

And so these practical movement experiences gradually establish a language of movement that is the basis of creative work in drama and dance.

Reasons for movement qualities

Simple ideas or reasons for moving in certain ways can now be introduced: for example, ask the children to move, as quietly as they can, anywhere in the hall. When they become really involved in this moving quietly, I should probably continue as follows:

You have been moving quietly because I asked you to. Now can you think of any reason for moving quietly without making a sound? Work out your own ideas and I will watch for the pictures you make.

This could be followed by a sequence of given movements: eg, moving quickly, stopping suddenly, and then moving slowly. Ask the children to repeat this pattern, trying to make clearer to themselves the variations of time; *feeling* from *inside* the sudden stop, the stillness, and the slow moving growing out of the stillness.

As they work with increasing inner effort, the movement sequence will become dramatic, and ideas will emerge. Now, encourage them to let their ideas take over, reminding them that every movement they make should help to build up their picture. They are now becoming more aware and appreciative of the qualities of movement, and simple situations can be given for the children to work out in their own ways: eg, moving through a wood without being seen; using stepping stones to cross a stream; crawling under a fence; looking for a gap in a hedge and forcing a way through; pushing open a heavy door and closing it quietly.

Adaptation to partners and groups

During these movement exercises, the children, while being aware of others moving around them, have been working individually. Through her own observations, the teacher will know when the time arrives for the children to work with others.

First let each child work with a partner. Start by asking them to walk together, looking for spaces, sensing changes of direction and speed without touching. Follow this by asking them to share a space with fingers lightly touching, making flowing shapes at different levels. Now they can share a space without touching, each child making his own shapes but being aware of his partner's movements. Now invite them to find different ways of meeting and leaving each other, such as coming together slowly, and leaving each other quickly. Out of these moving patterns, dramatic or dance forms may emerge. If this happens, encourage dramatic and dance development.

Now give them plenty of opportunity to explore definite situations that they can share and work out together: one helping the other across stepping stones; exploring a dark cave together; Bedivere helping the wounded King Arthur down to the lake.

Working in groups

After working with a partner, sharing a space, responding to another's movements, and sharing ideas, the child can begin to work in similar ways with increasing numbers.

1. Ask five or six children to share a space, weaving in and out at different levels, using varying speeds and movement qualities.

2. Ask them to walk around the hall, following a leader, feeling they are moving as a group, and avoiding contacts with other groups.

3. As their group feeling increases, encourage them to think of movement patterns: eg, making big, flowing movements, followed by a quick, downward movement; quickly forward, sudden stop, slowly backward. Encourage any resulting dramatic or dance form, giving time for development.

4. Let them move around with common feeling in their groups: eg, groups of frightened people, strong people, angry people, happy people. Develop these further by asking why they are moving in these ways. Give them time for discussion within their own groups so that they can work out their own situations.

5. Find out what happens when one group becomes aware of another group: eg, two groups meeting each other slowly; the meeting of two strong groups; the coming together of a weak and a strong group. Give time for discussion between the groups on resulting situations and working for further development.

6. Now give definite situations in which such groups are involved: eg, a meeting of groups of conspirators in the Gunpowder Plot; King Arthur and his followers facing Mordred and his men.

Sensitive observation and awareness give colour, shape and meaning to the world around us. To develop greater depth and feeling in expressive work, frequent opportunity must be given for sensory experiences and recalling of these experiences.

Handling of objects and materials from observation and discovery tables helps to pin-point the child's observation. Ask the children to pick up shells, fossils, pieces of wood, glass, cinders, pebbles; to look at their shape and colour in different lights, to feel and contrast their textures. After giving children time for delight in the handling of an object, ask them to recall their feelings in words or paint. Later, ask them to imagine that they are holding the shell, the piece of glass, etc. Can their eyes and their fingers recall the shape, texture, colour?

Ask them to perform various actions involving vivid sensory recall:

Put your hands into a bowl of sticky dough. Feel them sink in. Feel and watch the pull of the dough as you lift your hands out. Pull and scrape the dough from your fingers.

Think of a holly leaf. Let your fingers feel its smooth, glossy surface. Now touch its sharp, pointed prickles.

Think of snow. Watch the snowflakes falling, see how lightly they move. Feel them falling on your face, your hands. Watch them disappear as they melt on your hand. Let your feet sink into the snow. Can you feel and hear the crunch under your feet? Gather up some snow, feel its coldness. Press it firmly into snowballs. Feel the hardness and the shape.

Lie down. Imagine it is a warm, sunny day and you are lying on grass. Feel the warmth of the sun on your face, arms. Let your fingers touch the grass. Perhaps if you look carefully, you can see a ladybird on a blade of grass. Look at its colour as it moves. Hold out your hands. See if it will move onto your finger. Watch and feel it move on your hand and arm. Watch it disappear between the blades of grass. There is a sound overhead. What is it? A plane streaks across the sky leaving a white trail. Watch it disappear.

Think of King Arthur's sword. See it lying at your feet. Look at the length and strength of it, at the jewel-encrusted handle. Lift it carefully. Feel its weight. Move it around in different ways, watching the tip of it. Can you see the sparkle of the jewels as they catch the light? Feel the dryness of the rushes as you hide the sword on the edge of the lake. Hear the lapping of the water.

Characteriza-tion

During the exploring of personal space, the children will have had countless opportunities of finding out how their own bodies move. When the time is ripe, draw their attention to how other people move, and how the way they move depends on how they feel and on what sort of people they are.

1. Start by directing their attention to parts of their own bodies: eg, feet, hands:

   Feet *As you look at your feet, try to make them feel like the feet of an old man. How does this make the rest of your body feel? Move about inside this old man's body. Try to think like the old man. How does he speak? What does he talk about?*

   Hands *Look at your hands. Watch them grow into the greedy, grasping hands of Scrooge. What does this do to the rest of your body? How do you feel inside? What are your thoughts? Count your money, feeling like Scrooge.*

   They can be asked to make their shoulders those of a boastful or arrogant person, a timid or weak person; the head that of a proud person, and so on. Explore and experiment as with other parts.

2. Now try developing characterization from shape making.

   In your own space, grow into the sort of person who takes up a lot of space. Change to a person who takes up a little space. Try walking in these shapes.

   Think of a witch shape. Feel this shape from inside. Grow into it. Prepare your spells, keeping this shape. Talk to your cat.

   Make up your own character. Can you move in this shape, think in this shape? Can you meet another character and have a movement conversation, still keeping your shape?

3. Develop group characterization. Invite small groups, after discussion, to grow into the same sort of people, to walk about together, trying to keep the group character.
4. Start improvization. For example, take the theme of a family on the beach. The group discusses this situation. Then talk about the different people in the 'family'. They decide what sort of person each of them will be. They work out the situation.

Sound and movement leading to language flow

During all movement experiences, feeling is all important. As a child becomes more absorbed in his movements, there is continual searching for the right movements to express his feelings. The time comes when a child feels the need to communicate his experiences still further. Intense movement feeling develops into sounds expressing the same feeling. There is joy and life in this sound since it comes from within and is not imposed. Through further exploration, out of these sounds, come words and phrases leading to language expression, and natural communication that has vitality and flow.

1. At some point in 'shape-making', ask the children to concentrate on one movement shape: eg, a strong, straight movement. They should repeat this movement with increasing inner effort until they *feel* the sound that grows from it. Next they should let the sound accompany the movement, and then develop this sound into feeling a word, or phrase.

2. After this, get them to think of a word, feel it, say it, and let the movement come out with it: eg, 'explode', 'stealth', 'wonder', 'fireworks', and so on.

3. Start with a word or phrase and let it come out with *different* feeling and accompanying movements. For example, take the phrases 'Go away' and 'Come here', and suggest the children say them in a strong way, an imploring way, and a frightened way.

4. They can develop movement conversations with partners in the same way.

5. They can toss, flick, throw, and so on, movements from one partner to another, letting appropriate sounds develop.

6. They can experiment, sharing space and ideas with a partner, letting sounds, gibberish, and words develop.

7. Work with small groups in a similar way, for example, a group moving quietly. After they have moved together and felt movement quality, allow time for the group to discuss reasons for moving in this way, to bring ideas into their movement plan. As they work on their plan and feel the need to communicate still further with each other, sounds growing into words will follow.

8. Experiment further with characterization and improvisation, encouraging the children to let their sounds and words come from the movements, feelings, and thoughts of the character they are interpreting, eg,

   (a) Ask them to think of one of the strange creatures in *Jabberwocky*; to grow into the shape of the creature, move like it, think like it, feel like it, to feel the sounds that would come from it and let them come out with its movements.

(b) Two such creatures meet. Each child maintains his own characterization, with resulting movements, feelings and sounds. Two can then work on ideas arising from the meeting, and develop gibberish conversation.

(c) Three people meet: eg, three witches. The children assume witches' shapes, movements, sounds, etc, and develop ideas and language flow in this situation.

(d) Larger group improvisations are possible: eg, at the hairdresser's or barber's shop; groups round market stalls; a family picnic.

Here give time for defining individual characterizations before working out group improvisations.

The selection of the right words with the accompanying movement effort, the development of language flow between members of a group, will become a natural part of working out improvised situations and later will help to build up situations within dramatic themes.

Responding to external sounds and music

From an early stage in their movement experiences, children will respond readily to clear and direct sounds such as clapping, the beating of a drum, or the clash of cymbals. As they become more involved in movement qualities, as their sensitivity increases, they will respond to more subtle and varied percussion sounds, weaving patterns of movement that are either dance-like or dramatic.

Again, these movement sequences should develop from working individually to working with a partner and then with a group.

Careful choice of music is essential. From the beginning, children must have plenty of opportunity for listening and should be directly encouraged to listen.

I find that the most suitable music for an introduction to this listening and moving, is a simple tune with an easily recognized rhythm: eg, an English or Scottish country dance tune.

I ask the children to sit down and listen to the music. To direct their observation and concentration, I first ask them to let their hands 'listen' to it.

Make your hands listen to the music. Can they touch the floor, the space around and above you, while you are listening to it? Now let your head, fingers, shoulders, feet, listen to it. Can you feel it inside?

Now, on your feet, move in your own space, making every bit of yourself listen to the music. Can you still listen to the music and move around the hall?

Next come short musical passages with clear phrases, for shape-making. Here the children listen directly for phrases, feel them and interpret them in movement shapes: phrases that demand, for example, big, flowing movements, quick jerky movements, curling and uncurling shapes.

After working individually, the children work with partners and groups, finding ways of meeting and leaving, sharing a space, developing a pattern.

During these experiences, the children concentrate on rhythm, pattern, and shape of the music, and find their own way of interpretation. No dance techniques or steps are taught. These the children discover for themselves.

Frequently, we listen to music, concentrating on its mood and feeling. Here the selections are carefully chosen so that, over a period of time, the children have the opportunity of hearing music of many contrasting moods and feelings.

1. The children may interpret the mood suggested by the music, first by feeling it as they walk, and later by working out dramatic movement pictures suggested by the mood. Often these dramatic pictures are developed into group themes.

2. Sometimes characterization grows out of this listening.
3. Often music is selected in this way as a background for situations within dramatic themes that are being built up.

Working out a drama theme

After the children have explored the varied avenues of movement experience, the working out of dramatic themes with the entire class can be attempted. They now have a movement vocabulary, their movements are expressive and controlled, their imagination has been stimulated, and they have a sensitive awareness of individuals and the group.

Sources and materials for themes can be sparked off by some situation already worked out in movement; they may arise from the children's imaginative and creative writing; they may come from stories from literature, history, scripture, etc.

Whatever the source, all the children should be thoroughly immersed in the fabric of the theme and excited by the idea of working something out together.

There should be no definite or set plan to begin with. Gradually this will develop, as individual characterizations are drawn, situations and group reactions are worked out, and creative ideas are introduced through movement experiences.

Here we will consider how a theme could develop from THE PIED PIPER OF HAMELIN.

1. Read the poem for the enjoyment of the story.
2. Let children select and read aloud words, phrases, sentences that excite them, so that all the class can share in 'tasting' the colour and life of the words.
3. Now let them choose situations in the poem which they feel are dramatic and exciting.
4. Talk about the different feelings of individuals and groups within these situations—the changing attitudes and feelings as circumstances change.

5. Draw from the children their opinions of the different characters in the story. At this stage, the children will be eager to start working together.

6. Ask the children to move and feel as the harassed mayor who senses the townsfolk's anger, then as the jubilant mayor after the rats have disappeared; as the piper as he walks up the street; as a man or woman surveying the destruction caused by the rats; as the lame boy when he is left alone, and so on.

7. Work out situations in groups: the troubled councillors moving up the street; an angry crowd advancing towards the council chamber; rats creeping out at night; children following the piper. Contrast the group feeling of rejoicing when the rats have gone, with the sorrowing crowd when they realize their children have vanished for ever, and so on.

As the children become more absorbed, there will be increasing development in characterization, group feeling, and reaction. Ideas will grow within situations, sounds will come from movement, and the sounds will develop into speech.

At different stages in the working out, time should be given for observation of individuals and groups—followed by discussion and selection of the most dramatic interpretations.

A loose framework will then be drawn up and certain locations fixed: eg, the street, the council chamber, the river, the mountain.

In this framework the situations already worked out will be placed, and the theme will begin to take shape. As it develops, it may be felt that music could be introduced at some points to deepen the feeling: recorder music for the piper; FANTASIA ON A THEME OF THOMAS TALLIS (Vaughan Williams), as the rats creep out at night; NIGHT ON THE BARE MOUNTAIN (Mussorgsky), as the lame boy stands alone.

Since all the children will have explored all the characters, and will have shared in all the situations, they can at any time take any part, and at all times will act with real understanding in the situations and react sensitively to others around them.

The purpose of movement experience

Movement experience gives a child a remarkable control over his physical movements. It compels him to concentrate; it stimulates his imagination; it makes him react sensitively to other individuals and the group. As he explores and experiments with different qualities of movement, he develops powers of control and concentration. The more deeply he feels, the more his movements become an outward expression of his thoughts, feeling, and imagination. As his movements become more controlled, the more easily he moves. He lacks strain, and develops poise and awareness, becoming more sensitive and observant. As his concentration and absorption become deeper, he feels the need to communicate his experiences. He searches continually for the right movements, the right sounds and words. So, out of this sensitive awareness and observation, comes natural communication that is colourful, full of vitality and flow.

3 Drama in the Infant School

by Doris Nash

The importance of drama in contributing to the full development of children up to seven years of age is now widely accepted by teachers and parents. How this is achieved must depend on the sensitivity of the teacher and the skill she brings to daily working with young children. A few of the ways children have been helped are noted here—all from direct observation—in the hope that more children may be enabled to discover the exciting world of language—gesture—sound—communication.

Arrival at school Children, when they enter school as five-year-olds, take periods varying from two days to two months to adjust to the new situation of living and learning[1]—vastly different from preceding experience in home and street.

The skilled teacher's preparation of a room must include provision of a corner or large wood chest (at least 2 ft × 2 ft × 4 ft high) where a child can withdraw, alone or with a self-chosen friend.

It is in the private areas in the learning situation that the most exciting dramatic situations arise—always observed by the teacher, and guided by her, through provision of lengths of material for 'dressing-up', through her decision to equip this area as either a dramatic corner, or home corner, and so on. Observation of children in these private areas suggests that all children need such experiences. Language between child and child becomes much more precise. Here it is that persistent communications through gesture and head-nodding are noted.

[1]See, in this series, FROM HOME TO SCHOOL by Alice Murton

42

Encouraging speech

Once such communications have been noted, the teacher can contrive ways to encourage direct speech. Sometimes the dramatic corner itself is enough. However, if the child with a speech problem is sensitive and withdrawn, then many, many different ways may have to be tried before a response is found. Simple puppets have helped—one emotionally disturbed child was eventually prepared to use the puppet as a medium for speech, while still unable to speak directly to anyone.

Similarly, a child who had an uncontrolled voice and shouted everywhere learned self-control of his voice through making a puppet out of plastic containers.

In the group, a teacher can help a child gain control of his voice by sharing sound-making of vigorous quality—eg, wind roaring—with whole body movement, and gradually contrasting sounds with voice, or by blowing balloons or thistle-down. Children enjoy listening to adults using 'surprising voices', and once the child can listen, a whole new world of sound-making by the child—using stones and sticks, metals and air—opens up.

Exploring sound

The sensitive use of natural objects indoors and outdoors is an essential stage—though it should always be remembered that such experiences are just leading towards greater discoveries in quality of expressing speech and sounds.

Where does singing fit in most appropriately? Children, we know, have a great feeling for rhythm and sound. Watching a child in the dramatic corner, we note how sustained his breath-control is when he is mimicking a mother singing to a baby (the 'baby' may be anything from a doll to a roll of paper). The child's dramatic use of the material around indicates to an observant teacher: the imaginative child; the child who has no control of voice or gesture; the child with no ability to concentrate.

As the five-year-old develops and explores the

opportunities provided, the teacher is daily adding stories, well-read poems, and songs. She is deliberately adding words and sounds to help the child listen more carefully to, and communicate more easily with, peers and adults.

Many children come to school from a background of continuous sound of industry, radio, television, and traffic, and it is becoming increasingly difficult to achieve thoughtful listening. Only the teacher can determine whether a child needs the opportunity to listen to stories in isolation, in a small group, or in a large group.

Group situations

Manipulation of group situations by the child, through building, painting, dramatic play, excursions, and endless other experiences within the school, enables him to operate more fully. With more experiences and observation, children interpret and communicate in painting and language and movement. As in language at this stage, so much of what is creative is based on an experience or observation. The picture on the right shows life around the school, recorded in paint. Over seventy children painted something personally experienced, and their knowledge of space in movement and drama was here used in a creative presentation.

Children and teachers deliberately plan the outside area around the school to encourage observation. *All areas* are capable of exploitation.

In one, children have planted bulbs and saplings, and so have ceaseless opportunity for discussion, observation, and talking—even a handicapped child benefits (one of the children is a five-year-old mongol, living and sharing in a normal school day), contributing fully.

Structuring situations

Increasingly, the daily experiences within the school are structured by the teacher to obtain more precise and careful observation of growth and *shape* within and outside the building.

Plant growth fascinates children of six-plus years, who are sensitive to, and aware of, three-dimensional shape and pattern, both of which are so essential to drama.

Six-year-old children taken into the country for a day on a farm, use their earlier experiences of lifting, and are able to adapt to a real situation and move a heavy bale of hay. The farmer has a far greater skill, but the group of children solve the problem at their level of skill with such obvious enjoyment. (See the picture on page 46).

In spontaneous discussion in the classroom, following a story, children show animation, and desire to communicate and share their personal experiences. Notice the sensitive hand gestures. (See the picture on page 47.)

45

In the hall, children cluster around the teacher until they have experience of use of space. Many children are unwilling to undress, for several weeks after starting school. Some watch from the side until they have enough confidence in themselves and the teacher to explore movement more fully. (See the picture on page 48.)

(American readers may query some references in this booklet to children's undressing for movement. This means that boys and girls strip to the waist, the latter, at the onset of puberty, also wearing a vest or singlet. This goes back to 1933 when the Board (now the Department) of Education published a book of suggested exercises and activities involving headstands, cartwheels, climbing, etc. Hitherto, primary school children had done their physical exercises in their ordinary clothing which was exceedingly hampering to the kind of movement now required. Furthermore the problem of decency, so far as the girls were concerned, which had hardly existed in the old days of drill, became

self-evident. The girls' PE class in the early 1930s was often, to say the least of it, lacking in decorum.

Attempts by teachers to induce the girls to shed their skirts and to wear suitable pants were, in the early days, resisted by many parents and, when the boys stripped to the waist, their mothers frequently feared for their chests. Gradually common sense prevailed, parents saw the reasonableness of what was being done and the practice is now general, if not universal.)

Gaining confidence, the child will gradually become aware of his entire body. He will start moving at low levels, using space and speed and direction with concentrated thinking and effort, making self-disciplined movements.

Five-year-old girls use junk material to make

puppets. The teacher will use the puppets for direct communication with the girls as *one* way into drama. (See the picture on page 49.)

Some children's records

This section contains the ideas of seven-year-old children as expressed by them.

How children record experience
It seems important to note how much the environment conditioned by the teachers, becomes part of the child's dramatic and recorded language. Some

children record in speech, in singing, in movement, in paint, in clay. Children need freedom to select *their* most creative way of recording.

For example, Marie, unable to achieve academic success, inspired and influenced the entire group through her sensitive movement and her choice of a gay golden gown. Simon, with a sung tune, and creative use of voice and body, inspired music and language.

We have learned that children are able to extend an original idea (they seldom if ever enlarge or change the idea), and each development complements the preceding episode—any number of children can be accommodated and the children show respect for any creative effort.

Discipline appears to be maintained by them through: music, recorded or sung; language, spoken or sung; movement, gesture and mime.

They have ability to group themselves as the drama demands—a very sensitive awareness of periods of repose following vigorous movement or sound. These qualities seem part of a seven-year-old's skill in drama.

The criterion for teacher and child, must be absorbed happiness, reflected in dramatic movement and individual creative interpretation. (See the picture below.)

After many such experiences, we see how children's own written records reflect the impact drama has on the young child.

Children's records

Words, tune and movement sequence by Simon:

GG A# A# A D GG A# A# AA A CCC A# G CCCC A# G.

In the moonlit sky
A lightning dragon came
with a flutter of a wing.
It was morning again
and with a mysterious swirl
He rose into the sunlit sky.

In the dreary mist
A blue-winged, green-backed dragon
came swirling in curves
His way out of his cave,
and with a mighty flap
He rose into the moonlit sky.

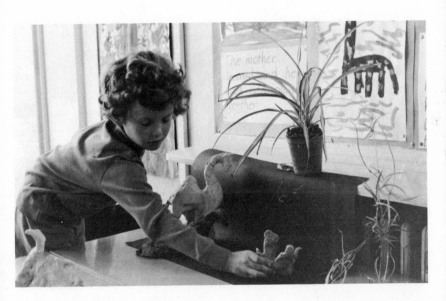

Crying Spell by Sarah Jane (words, music and dance):

Crying . . . crying . . . crying . . . crying . . .

(This dance sequence reminded adults of Greek drama.)

51

By Graham:

At school after dinner all the girls go in the hall and they dress up in gowns. When I do my spell it is broken by a laughing spell. We do lovely movements when we are in the hall . . . some boys join in and they are horsemen.

By Dean:

During the dinner-hour I go in the hall to do the Play—we had to wear a cloak and we have to get in position and then the horseman start to gallop and then the horseman go back to the stable and the horseman lie down because the music stops—the music is the tambourine—the musicians used little shoes to make the sound of the hooves hitting the ground.

Laughing Spell by Victoria (words and tune):

Abracadabra Ha! Ha! Ha!
   Abracadabra He! He! He!
Wherever I go I dance with glee!
   Abracadabra He! He! He!
This is my sung spell.

We do all kinds of spells in our school hall. We play instruments for our spells. There are about forty people in our hall with spells—not all of the people have got spells.

We do our play nearly every day now—the instruments we use are called chime bars and a xylophone.

Spell by Paul:

In this school we do a play and we have a wizard in the play and the wizard has a spell, it is
   'My magic, my magic,
      Her magic, her magic,

Oh Wizard, OH WIZARD!'
These words are the words of the wizard's spell that she sings while she is dancing about, and when she casts her spell everybody near her goes to sleep.

And we have a spell called 'Fiddle de ree':
'Fiddle de ree, the magic of the night
 Fiddle de ree, the moon we see,
Fiddle de ree, a silver sphere,
 Fiddle de ree, an upturned boat,
Fiddle de ree, as black as a cat.'

These words are the words of the spell and it makes two cats dance around the room.

By John:
In our play I am a creature and there are seven more and we try to break the spell and some of us are kangaroos and I am a tiger and we go about on the floor and we do some long movements and we do some nice movements and we go around the moonbeams and we go in between the boxes and we go around fast and the moonbeams move us away.

Words and Dance Sequence by Ruth:

Blue I am
Blue as mist
 Swirling softly
Over clouds.
Blue I am
 Blue as mist.

In the play I sing this song and while I sing the song I do movement and I swirl and turn and lift my skirt and look as though I am floating in the air and Frank is the blue-winged green-backed dragon and Simon is a blue-winged green-backed dragon too and Debbie is the wind dragon and she does movement like me and she wears a yellow skirt and I wear a green skirt.

For this particular drama by Ruth, movement

came first—then came the words. The tune was composed by another child, and eventually the words were sung as Ruth controlled a group of children during lunch-hour drama—either in the hall or out in the field. Dramatic communication, at this age, is never finished.

It should be noted how the growing awareness of other children in the group comes through clearly in the child's own writing.

By Christopher:

Lorry driver you're big and strong
Going faster and faster as you go along
*   past trees and houses early in the morning*
And you see the grass heavy with dew
And making magnificent patterns.

By Murray:

On the desolate sands the seagulls scampered
And left footprints small and footprints thin
I walked along and I heard them screeching
And when I got near they flew away.

By Neil:

The roaring waves hurtled upon the shore
But when it got dark the waves went down
*   When we went to see the boats*
They bobbed up and down gently.

By Susan:

I heard the wind roaring through the trees
*   The angry voice of the wind on the sea*
I saw the waves tossing and turning
*   And running quickly back to me.*
I climbed some rocks to find some pools
*   The rocks were very pointed*
I saw a crab—it was moving quickly
*   Trying to get out of the pool.*

By Fiona:

We went to a wild-life park
Where I saw some lovely swans
They stretched their necks and made themselves
tall

And it was quite windy.
All the trees were waving happily
Bending over a river was a big willow tree.

By David:

Noise
I like noise
The thud of a hoof
The clang of a door
And the crash of a train.

By Debra:

The Howling of the Wind
The howling wind blows through the open tree-tops
The rain pours through the tree like thunder
It rattles through the rain-pipes hurriedly.

By Mark:

Sounds I like
The crunching of leaves in Autumn
The chime-bars ringing
The growling of a motor-bike racing
The glide of birds flying swiftly through the air.
The pattering of rain on a roof.
These are the sounds
I like to hear.

Instruments, and sticks and stones used in rhythms, as well as the teacher's sensitivity in use of voice, contribute to children's awareness of sound.

By Elaine:

When we do movement we do all different kinds of things. Sometimes we do circular movements and sometimes we do sharp short movements—sometimes we do twisty movements. Mrs Patterson sometimes asks us to relax and then she says a strong shape—now! We curl and then we let go and sometimes we move along like that.

You can speak with somebody by moving your arm in the direction you want them to go. You can make up a story in movement. I shared my story with Pippy and Jane—in our story we were witches and we were trying to make other people into witches.

Elaine's writing, I feel, reflects how important the relationship between teacher and child is. I do not expect many seven-year-old children to be capable of self-analysis. (See the picture below.)

By Vivian:

Happy birds fly everywhere . . .
That is the beginning of my poem and Elizabeth
plays for me and the instrument she uses is the tubular
instrument and it has a bell noise and it has the right
sound for my bird poem and I like the sound because it
has a jingle in the sound and it sounds like birds
chattering and I like the music which Elizabeth plays
for me and I read my poem while Elizabeth plays.

Happy birds fly everywhere
We never know where
But when the blackbird sings his song
We know he's very near.

And when we look at the long, long grass
We know the pheasants come here
Above the grass I see his head
He looks so beautiful and big.

Then we go to the dark dark wood.
We find the tree creepers here
Then when the dark falls on us
We hear the owls loud hoot!

Composed by five children and used to control
forty children in the drama:

Search the curving branches of the leafless tree
Search the cracking bending bough
Hear the rumbles of the storm
Hear the roaring of the wind
See the angry clouds so grey
See them sweep across the sky
Watch the twisty willow bend
Watch the gliding of the birds.

Search the secrets of the snow
See the crook shaped icicles
See the foot print of a fox
Feel the bitter bitter wind
Feel the softness of the snow

By Sarah Jane:

At school in the lunch-hour the girls go into the hall and do a play. The play has got spells in it. I am in the play and have got a spell. My spell makes the girls cry. Boys come into the hall and they are horsemen.

When I have done my spell someone else does their spell. I like doing the play.

When we have done the play we put our gowns away. My gown is mauve. My spell is sad. (See the picture below.)

David's story of a ballet:

I am a moonbeam in our play. We come from a crowd of little planets: the planets are really six boxes in a circle.

The other people are—king, queen, prince, lots of

princesses, four prison workers, a cloudy witch, two thunder witches.

The new climbing apparatus is the castle where the Prince lives. The big grey mattress is the thunder-cloud—the small blue mattress is a lake.

The witches want to keep the Princesses from the castle, so they can live in the castle instead of their thunder clouds—when people are forced to trip on the mattress by the witch you are dead. The witch does not touch you—she does the movement of pushing.

We dance to the music of Bach—there are two pieces of music the moonbeams do not dance to—the other children dance to them.

After their pieces they go to sleep and we come down from our planets to search for the castle in the clouds. When we find it we wake them all up after their deep sleep. It takes quite a time to do this. I go up on a planet and make the movement of two circles with my arms. Then they get into groups and do a dance.

Drama, a unifying influence

How does drama help a child to represent his learning more completely?

From our many observations of children, we are aware that once a child in infant school understands how to place himself in 'space' in relationship to other members of a group,[1] then other things follow. For such understanding expresses a certain level of conceptualization, of thinking, which becomes part of a child, and which permits a teacher thereafter to expect this quality to be expressed in all areas of this child's learning.

Preparation

In her movement periods, the teacher will quite deliberately help this quality to develop on the basis of her specific knowledge of a child's needs. This will involve the teacher in concentrated preparation before the lesson. She will not only need to plan the language and quality of movement she knows she can expect from her group, but she must understand young children's need for self-disciplined movement in restricted areas as well as

[1]See Bess Bullough's essay in this booklet

for expansive movement.

Language will be used only to inspire the children to think for themselves, translating it into terms of whole body movement, and enabling them to make instant decisions. This is essential; for each child has his own rhythm, and the teacher must allow for each child to experiment with this rhythm. Instructions, too, must be phrased to permit each child his unique interpretation. It is not enough, for example, to ask children to 'move'. Until a child knows quality of speed, and understands direction, and levels of movement, as well as space, he cannot fully interpret such an instruction, and the period becomes occupational rather than educational.

Confidence

When a child has awareness of and skill and confidence in body movements, in relation to the group environment, then this is reflected:

1. in his general attitude to all school situations and the ability to share his learning with adults and children;
2. in his painting—particularly in spacing of colour and design on paper;
3. in arrangements of 3-dimensional objects in space—working either in isolation or with his selected group (the objects being selected and arranged to show the growing ability to discriminate, and see relationships):
   (a) shapes in clay—made by children
   (b) shapes in wood—found by children
   (c) solid glass shapes linking directly with precise mathematical language.
   (d) shapes in colour
   (e) skeleton shapes
   (f) fossil shapes
   (g) growing shapes, and so on
   (the choice is endless, and is only valuable when related to the all-round development of the child),

4. in presentation of his work in an interesting and exciting way.

Contact with the teacher

Teachers of five-year-old children will be aware from their own observations that most children at this stage of growth will need a close contact with the teacher—and may be quite unable to explore even the environment of the classroom without adult support. These children must be given confidence and time to develop their own rhythms—even though the teacher may wish them to 'join in fully'. I have seen five-year-olds just 'watching' from the fringe of the group for even a term.

If the *rapport* between teacher and child is related to a child's individual need, the child will be absorbing and learning. To date I have not encountered a child who did not eventually join in.

Even a six-year-old, in a new situation, must have time to adjust to a new teacher and new peers, before he is able to use his thinking fully in movement and drama situations. The skilled teacher gives extra opportunities but no pressures until the child is adjusted.

Watching can be an essential part of absorbed learning for both child and teacher. In fact, watching and listening by the teacher is an essential part of her preparation of the environment. The more we observe children, the more we realize how learning must relate to the total child.

Ways to creativity

While it is quite impossible to determine which of them should come first in a child's experience, enough observations have been made to show that any of the following can help a child to a creative experience:

1. listening to music, stories and poetry;
2. gaining skill in gesture;
3. making rhythmic patterns with natural things;
4. making tunes on musical instruments;

5. making puppets;
6. awareness of textures, and observation;
7. thought for other people—adults and children;
8. props, costumes sometimes help, sometimes
    impede movements.

These are some of the ways into drama, for young children. But how does drama, this specific experience, become generalized, and lead to learning in other areas?

A unifying experience
The effect of drama on the daily life of a school can be noted. Most important, the creative uses of dramatic experiences are reflected in the language of the children. (One can discover in the children's vocabulary in the examples quoted earlier, the influences of T. S. Eliot, John Clare and James Reeves, among others.) In addition, the staff's thinking is clearly influenced by the experience. Being open-ended, communication between children and adults is continuous—sharpening thinking, and enabling concepts to be formed.

Moreover, the actual use of the language—in other words talking and listening—is essential to all children's full development. Children who don't talk, or whose experience in talking either to adults or their peers is limited, will have extra difficulty in learning to read.

Finally, recording and writing are expected when appropriate. For only when a child is fully aware of himself within the class community, and is thinking for himself, can we reasonably expect that communication through the written word will be well presented. And all children can present their own work in an interesting way, whatever their academic limitations.

Thus drama enables a child to represent his learning and understanding to others in many different ways. In particular, it gives a child extra confidence in dealing with day-to-day problems of growing up. In effect, drama unifies the total child.

Booklist

Garrard, Alan and Wiles, John LEAP TO LIFE—AN EXPERIMENT IN YOUTH DRAMA Chatto & Windus, London 1969

Haggerty, J. PLEASE MISS CAN I PLAY GOD? Methuen, London 1966

Way, Brian DEVELOPMENT THROUGH DRAMA Longman, London 1971; Humanities Press, New York 1971

See also the following booklets in this series: AN INTRODUCTION, ENVIRONMENTAL STUDIES, TOWARDS INFORMALITY, MUSIC, THE PUPIL'S DAY.

Audio-Visual Aids

FREE TO MOVE
This is a 16 mm colour film which runs for 35 minutes. It was made for the Schools Council by Southern Film Productions and is available in England from: Southern Film Productions, Brockenhurst Film Studios, Brockenhurst, Hants SO4 7RD, and in the USA from: The Film/Play Data Bureau Inc., 267 W. 25th Street, New York, NY.

MOVEMENT IN TIME AND SPACE
A black and white film which runs for 30 minutes. It is available in England from National Audio Visual Aids Library, Paxton Place, Gipsy Road, London S.E.27, and in the USA from: Time-Life Films, 43 West 16th Street, New York, NY 10011.

Glossary

For a fuller understanding of some terms that are briefly defined in the following list, the reader is referred to one or more books in this series.

Cooperative teaching
Team teaching. An example of cooperative teaching is described in detail in A RURAL SCHOOL.

Eleven plus (11+)
Term used to cover the procedures and techniques (eg, attainment and/or intelligence tests, and teachers' reports) used by local education authorities mainly to select pupils for grammar schools at the age of 11; formerly in universal use, now decreasingly, and only in areas where selection continues. A view of the eleven plus is given in AN INTRODUCTION by Joseph Featherstone.

Family grouping
See **Vertical grouping**.

Grammar school
Academic High School.

Half-term
Mid-semester (see also **Term**).

Hall
Multi-purpose space, large enough to hold the whole school (staff and pupils). Usually a large room, often combining the functions of dining hall, auditorium and gymnasium.

Headteacher
Principal. For an examination of the headteacher's work, and the differences between headteachers and US principals, see THE HEADTEACHER'S ROLE and THE GOVERNMENT OF EDUCATION.

Health visitor
Qualified nurse with special training who is employed by the local education authority to visit schools to check on the children's health.

Her Majesty's Inspector (HMI)
Her Majesty's Inspector of Schools. Appointed formally by the Privy Council to advise the Department of Education and Science, and schools, on the practices and standards of education; and to maintain liaison between the DES and local education authorities. See also THE GOVERNMENT OF EDUCATION.

Infant school	School or department for children from five to seven or eight years old.
Integrated day	A school day in which children may pursue various interests or themes, without regard to artificial divisions into time periods. The workings of an integrated day are fully described in A RURAL SCHOOL.
Junior school	School for seven to eleven or twelve year olds.
Local education authority (LEA)	County or county borough council with responsibility for public education in its area. See THE GOVERNMENT OF EDUCATION.
Movement	An activity where the children explore expressive, agile, and games-like situations. This is done through the dynamic use of the body, with spatial orientation as it comes into contact with people and objects.
Primary school	School for children under twelve. It may be an **Infant school** or **Junior school** (*qq.v.*) or a combination of both.
School managers	Members of an appointed managing body of not fewer than six members who are representative of various interests concerned with the school. For a fuller explanation, and information on the powers and responsibilities of school managers, see THE GOVERNMENT OF EDUCATION.
School year	This begins in September and consists of three terms (see **Terms**).
Special classes	Remedial classes.
Standards I-VIII	Grades in the former Elementary Schools (for children from five to fourteen years).
Streaming	Tracking.
Teachers' centre	A centre set up by a local education authority to provide opportunities for curriculum development and associated in-service training for teachers. See EDUCATING TEACHERS.
Term	The English school year is divided into three terms (cf semesters): Autumn (Fall), Spring, and Summer.
Timetable	Schedule.
Tuition	Teaching. (In Britain, the word 'tuition' never has the meaning, 'fees'.)
Vertical grouping	(also called **Family grouping**): Form of grouping, found mainly in infant schools, in which the full age range for which the school provides may be represented in each class. See also SPACE, TIME AND GROUPING.